REAL ESTATE
Log Book

This book belongs to:

_____

_____

_____

Individual Real Estate Log

Name: _____ **Date:** _____

Phone Number: _____ **Email:** _____

Address: _____

Budget: _____ **Deposit:** _____

Preferred Location		Property Needs	

Viewed	Suitable Properties

Notes: _____

_____

_____

_____

_____

_____

Property Sold	Costs	
	VALUE	
	SOLD FOR	
	COMMISSION	

Individual Real Estate Log

Name: _____ Date: _____

Phone Number: _____ Email: _____

Address: _____

Budget: _____ Deposit: _____

Preferred Location		Property Needs	

Viewed	Suitable Properties

Notes: _____

_____

_____

_____

_____

Property Sold	Costs	
	VALUE	
	SOLD FOR	
	COMMISSION	

Individual Real Estate Log

Name: _____ Date: _____

Phone Number: _____ Email: _____

Address: _____

_____

Budget: _____ Deposit: _____

Preferred Location		Property Needs	

Viewed	Suitable Properties

Notes: _____

_____

_____

_____

_____

_____

Property Sold	Costs	
	VALUE	
	SOLD FOR	
	COMMISSION	

Individual Real Estate Log

Name: _____ Date: _____
Phone Number: _____ Email: _____
Address: _____
_____

Budget: _____ Deposit: _____

Preferred Location		Property Needs	

Viewed	Suitable Properties

Notes: _____
_____
_____
_____
_____
_____

Property Sold	Costs	
	VALUE	
	SOLD FOR	
	COMMISSION	

Individual Real Estate Log

Name: _____ Date: _____

Phone Number: _____ Email: _____

Address: _____

_____

Budget: _____ Deposit: _____

Preferred Location		Property Needs	

Viewed	Suitable Properties

Notes: _____

_____

_____

_____

_____

_____

Property Sold	Costs	
	VALUE	
	SOLD FOR	
	COMMISSION	

Individual Real Estate Log

Name: _____ Date: _____

Phone Number: _____ Email: _____

Address: _____

_____

Budget: _____ Deposit: _____

Preferred Location		Property Needs	

Viewed	Suitable Properties

Notes: _____

_____

_____

_____

_____

Property Sold	Costs	
	VALUE	
	SOLD FOR	
	COMMISSION	

Individual Real Estate Log

Name: _____ Date: _____

Phone Number: _____ Email: _____

Address: _____

Budget: _____ Deposit: _____

Preferred Location		Property Needs	

Viewed	Suitable Properties

Notes: _____

_____

_____

_____

_____

_____

Property Sold	Costs	
	VALUE	
	SOLD FOR	
	COMMISSION	

Individual Real Estate Log

Name: _____ Date: _____
Phone Number: _____ Email: _____
Address: _____
_____

Budget: _____ Deposit: _____

Preferred Location		Property Needs	

Viewed	Suitable Properties

Notes: _____
_____
_____
_____
_____
_____

Property Sold	Costs	
	VALUE	
	SOLD FOR	
	COMMISSION	

Individual Real Estate Log

Name: _____ Date: _____

Phone Number: _____ Email: _____

Address: _____

_____

Budget: _____ Deposit: _____

Preferred Location		Property Needs	

Viewed	Suitable Properties

Notes: _____

_____

_____

_____

_____

_____

Property Sold	Costs	
	VALUE	
	SOLD FOR	
	COMMISSION	

Individual Real Estate Log

Name: _____ Date: _____

Phone Number: _____ Email: _____

Address: _____

_____

Budget: _____ Deposit: _____

Preferred Location		Property Needs	

Viewed	Suitable Properties

Notes: _____

_____

_____

_____

_____

Property Sold	Costs	
	VALUE	
	SOLD FOR	
	COMMISSION	

Individual Real Estate Log

Name: _____ Date: _____

Phone Number: _____ Email: _____

Address: _____
_____

Budget: _____ Deposit: _____

Preferred Location		Property Needs	

Viewed	Suitable Properties

Notes: _____
_____
_____
_____
_____
_____

Property Sold	Costs	
	VALUE	
	SOLD FOR	
	COMMISSION	

Individual Real Estate Log

Name: _____ **Date:** _____

Phone Number: _____ **Email:** _____

Address: _____

Budget: _____ **Deposit:** _____

Preferred Location		Property Needs	

Viewed	Suitable Properties

Notes: _____

_____

_____

_____

_____

_____

Property Sold	Costs	
	VALUE	
	SOLD FOR	
	COMMISSION	

Individual Real Estate Log

Name: _____ Date: _____

Phone Number: _____ Email: _____

Address: _____

_____

Budget: _____ Deposit: _____

Preferred Location		Property Needs	

Viewed	Suitable Properties

Notes: _____

_____

_____

_____

_____

_____

Property Sold	Costs	
	VALUE	
	SOLD FOR	
	COMMISSION	

Individual Real Estate Log

Name: _____ Date: _____

Phone Number: _____ Email: _____

Address: _____
_____

Budget: _____ Deposit: _____

Preferred Location		Property Needs	

Viewed	Suitable Properties

Notes: _____
_____
_____
_____
_____

Property Sold	Costs	
	VALUE	
	SOLD FOR	
	COMMISSION	

Individual Real Estate Log

Name: _____ Date: _____

Phone Number: _____ Email: _____

Address: _____

Budget: _____ Deposit: _____

Preferred Location		Property Needs	

Viewed	Suitable Properties

Notes: _____

_____

_____

_____

_____

_____

Property Sold		Costs
	VALUE	
	SOLD FOR	
	COMMISSION	

Individual Real Estate Log

Name:_____ Date:_____

Phone Number:_____ Email:_____

Address:_____

_____

Budget:_____ Deposit:_____

Preferred Location		Property Needs	

Viewed	Suitable Properties

Notes:_____

_____

_____

_____

_____

Property Sold	Costs	
	VALUE	
	SOLD FOR	
	COMMISSION	

Individual Real Estate Log

Name: _____ Date: _____

Phone Number: _____ Email: _____

Address: _____

_____

Budget: _____ Deposit: _____

Preferred Location		Property Needs	

Viewed	Suitable Properties

Notes: _____

_____

_____

_____

_____

_____

Property Sold	Costs	
	VALUE	
	SOLD FOR	
	COMMISSION	

Individual Real Estate Log

Name: _____ Date: _____

Phone Number: _____ Email: _____

Address: _____
_____

Budget: _____ Deposit: _____

Preferred Location		Property Needs	

Viewed	Suitable Properties

Notes: _____
_____
_____
_____
_____
_____

Property Sold	Costs	
	VALUE	
	SOLD FOR	
	COMMISSION	

Individual Real Estate Log

Name: _____ Date: _____

Phone Number: _____ Email: _____

Address: _____

_____

Budget: _____ Deposit: _____

Preferred Location		Property Needs	

Viewed	Suitable Properties

Notes: _____

_____

_____

_____

_____

_____

Property Sold	Costs	
	VALUE	
	SOLD FOR	
	COMMISSION	

Individual Real Estate Log

Name: _____ Date: _____

Phone Number: _____ Email: _____

Address: _____

Budget: _____ Deposit: _____

Preferred Location		Property Needs	

Viewed	Suitable Properties

Notes: _____

_____

_____

_____

_____

Property Sold	Costs	
	VALUE	
	SOLD FOR	
	COMMISSION	

Individual Real Estate Log

Name: _____ Date: _____

Phone Number: _____ Email: _____

Address: _____

_____

Budget: _____ Deposit: _____

Preferred Location		Property Needs	

Viewed	Suitable Properties

Notes: _____

_____

_____

_____

_____

_____

Property Sold	Costs	
	VALUE	
	SOLD FOR	
	COMMISSION	

Individual Real Estate Log

Name: _____ Date: _____

Phone Number: _____ Email: _____

Address: _____

_____

Budget: _____ Deposit: _____

Preferred Location		Property Needs	

Viewed	Suitable Properties

Notes: _____

_____

_____

_____

_____

_____

Property Sold	Costs	
	VALUE	
	SOLD FOR	
	COMMISSION	

Individual Real Estate Log

Name: _____ Date: _____

Phone Number: _____ Email: _____

Address: _____

_____

Budget: _____ Deposit: _____

Preferred Location		Property Needs	

Viewed	Suitable Properties

Notes: _____

_____

_____

_____

_____

_____

Property Sold	Costs	
	VALUE	
	SOLD FOR	
	COMMISSION	

Individual Real Estate Log

Name: _____ Date: _____

Phone Number: _____ Email: _____

Address: _____

_____

Budget: _____ Deposit: _____

Preferred Location		Property Needs	

Viewed	Suitable Properties

Notes: _____

_____

_____

_____

_____

_____

Property Sold	Costs	
	VALUE	
	SOLD FOR	
	COMMISSION	

Individual Real Estate Log

Name: _____ **Date:** _____

Phone Number: _____ **Email:** _____

Address: _____

Budget: _____ **Deposit:** _____

Preferred Location		Property Needs	

Viewed	Suitable Properties

Notes: _____
_____
_____
_____
_____
_____

Property Sold	Costs	
	VALUE	
	SOLD FOR	
	COMMISSION	

Individual Real Estate Log

Name: _____ Date: _____

Phone Number: _____ Email: _____

Address: _____

Budget: _____ Deposit: _____

Preferred Location		Property Needs	

Viewed	Suitable Properties

Notes: _____
_____
_____
_____
_____
_____
_____

Property Sold	Costs	
	VALUE	
	SOLD FOR	
	COMMISSION	

Individual Real Estate Log

Name: _____ **Date:** _____

Phone Number: _____ **Email:** _____

Address: _____

Budget: _____ **Deposit:** _____

Preferred Location		Property Needs	

Viewed	Suitable Properties

Notes: _____

_____

_____

_____

_____

_____

Property Sold	Costs	
	VALUE	
	SOLD FOR	
	COMMISSION	

Individual Real Estate Log

Name: _____ Date: _____

Phone Number: _____ Email: _____

Address: _____

_____

Budget: _____ Deposit: _____

Preferred Location		Property Needs	

Viewed	Suitable Properties

Notes: _____

_____

_____

_____

_____

Property Sold	Costs	
	VALUE	
	SOLD FOR	
	COMMISSION	

Individual Real Estate Log

Name: _____ Date: _____

Phone Number: _____ Email: _____

Address: _____

_____

Budget: _____ Deposit: _____

Preferred Location		Property Needs	

Viewed	Suitable Properties

Notes: _____

_____

_____

_____

_____

_____

Property Sold	Costs	
	VALUE	
	SOLD FOR	
	COMMISSION	

Individual Real Estate Log

Name: _____ Date: _____

Phone Number: _____ Email: _____

Address: _____

Budget: _____ Deposit: _____

Preferred Location		Property Needs	

Viewed	Suitable Properties

Notes: _____

_____

_____

_____

_____

_____

Property Sold	Costs	
	VALUE	
	SOLD FOR	
	COMMISSION	

Individual Real Estate Log

Name: _____ **Date:** _____

Phone Number: _____ **Email:** _____

Address: _____

_____

Budget: _____ **Deposit:** _____

Preferred Location		Property Needs	

Viewed	Suitable Properties

Notes: _____

_____

_____

_____

_____

_____

Property Sold	Costs	
	VALUE	
	SOLD FOR	
	COMMISSION	

Individual Real Estate Log

Name: _____ **Date:** _____

Phone Number: _____ **Email:** _____

Address: _____

_____

Budget: _____ **Deposit:** _____

Preferred Location		Property Needs	

Viewed	Suitable Properties

Notes: _____

_____

_____

_____

_____

_____

Property Sold	Costs	
	VALUE	
	SOLD FOR	
	COMMISSION	

Individual Real Estate Log

Name: _____ Date: _____

Phone Number: _____ Email: _____

Address: _____
_____

Budget: _____ Deposit: _____

Preferred Location		Property Needs	

Viewed	Suitable Properties

Notes: _____
_____
_____
_____
_____
_____

Property Sold	Costs	
	VALUE	
	SOLD FOR	
	COMMISSION	

Individual Real Estate Log

Name: _____ Date: _____

Phone Number: _____ Email: _____

Address: _____
_____

Budget: _____ Deposit: _____

Preferred Location		Property Needs	

Viewed	Suitable Properties

Notes: _____
_____
_____
_____
_____
_____

Property Sold	Costs	
	VALUE	
	SOLD FOR	
	COMMISSION	

Individual Real Estate Log

Name: _____ Date: _____

Phone Number: _____ Email: _____

Address: _____

_____

Budget: _____ Deposit: _____

Preferred Location		Property Needs	

Viewed	Suitable Properties

Notes: _____

_____

_____

_____

_____

_____

Property Sold	Costs	
	VALUE	
	SOLD FOR	
	COMMISSION	

Individual Real Estate Log

Name: _____ Date: _____

Phone Number: _____ Email: _____

Address: _____

Budget: _____ Deposit: _____

Preferred Location		Property Needs	

Viewed	Suitable Properties

Notes: _____

_____

_____

_____

_____

Property Sold	Costs	
	VALUE	
	SOLD FOR	
	COMMISSION	

Individual Real Estate Log

Name: _____ Date: _____

Phone Number: _____ Email: _____

Address: _____

_____

Budget: _____ Deposit: _____

Preferred Location		Property Needs	

Viewed	Suitable Properties

Notes: _____

_____

_____

_____

_____

_____

Property Sold	Costs	
	VALUE	
	SOLD FOR	
	COMMISSION	

Individual Real Estate Log

Name: _____ **Date:** _____

Phone Number: _____ **Email:** _____

Address: _____

Budget: _____ **Deposit:** _____

Preferred Location		Property Needs	

Viewed	Suitable Properties

Notes: _____

_____

_____

_____

_____

_____

Property Sold	Costs	
	VALUE	
	SOLD FOR	
	COMMISSION	

Individual Real Estate Log

Name: _____ Date: _____

Phone Number: _____ Email: _____

Address: _____

_____

Budget: _____ Deposit: _____

Preferred Location		Property Needs	

Viewed	Suitable Properties

Notes: _____

_____

_____

_____

_____

_____

Property Sold	Costs	
	VALUE	
	SOLD FOR	
	COMMISSION	

Individual Real Estate Log

Name:_____ Date:_____

Phone Number:_____ Email:_____

Address:_____

_____

Budget:_____ Deposit:_____

Preferred Location		Property Needs	

Viewed	Suitable Properties

Notes:_____

_____

_____

_____

_____

_____

Property Sold	Costs	
	VALUE	
	SOLD FOR	
	COMMISSION	

Individual Real Estate Log

Name: _____ Date: _____

Phone Number: _____ Email: _____

Address: _____

_____

Budget: _____ Deposit: _____

Preferred Location		Property Needs	

Viewed	Suitable Properties

Notes: _____

_____

_____

_____

_____

_____

Property Sold		Costs
	VALUE	
	SOLD FOR	
	COMMISSION	

Individual Real Estate Log

Name: _____ **Date:** _____

Phone Number: _____ **Email:** _____

Address: _____
_____

Budget: _____ **Deposit:** _____

Preferred Location		Property Needs	

Viewed	Suitable Properties

Notes: _____
_____
_____
_____
_____
_____

Property Sold	Costs	
	VALUE	
	SOLD FOR	
	COMMISSION	

Individual Real Estate Log

Name: _____ Date: _____

Phone Number: _____ Email: _____

Address: _____
_____

Budget: _____ Deposit: _____

Preferred Location		Property Needs	

Viewed	Suitable Properties

Notes: _____
_____
_____
_____
_____
_____

Property Sold		Costs
	VALUE	
	SOLD FOR	
	COMMISSION	

Individual Real Estate Log

Name: _____ Date: _____

Phone Number: _____ Email: _____

Address: _____

Budget: _____ Deposit: _____

Preferred Location		Property Needs	

Viewed	Suitable Properties

Notes: _____

_____

_____

_____

_____

_____

Property Sold	Costs	
	VALUE	
	SOLD FOR	
	COMMISSION	

Individual Real Estate Log

Name: _____ Date: _____

Phone Number: _____ Email: _____

Address: _____

_____

Budget: _____ Deposit: _____

Preferred Location		Property Needs	

Viewed	Suitable Properties

Notes: _____

_____

_____

_____

_____

_____

Property Sold	Costs	
	VALUE	
	SOLD FOR	
	COMMISSION	

Individual Real Estate Log

Name: _____ **Date:** _____

Phone Number: _____ **Email:** _____

Address: _____

Budget: _____ **Deposit:** _____

Preferred Location		Property Needs	

Viewed	Suitable Properties

Notes: _____

_____

_____

_____

_____

Property Sold	Costs	
	VALUE	
	SOLD FOR	
	COMMISSION	

Individual Real Estate Log

Name: _____ **Date:** _____

Phone Number: _____ **Email:** _____

Address: _____

_____

Budget: _____ **Deposit:** _____

Preferred Location		Property Needs	

Viewed	Suitable Properties

Notes: _____

_____

_____

_____

_____

_____

Property Sold	Costs	
	VALUE	
	SOLD FOR	
	COMMISSION	

Individual Real Estate Log

Name: _____ Date: _____

Phone Number: _____ Email: _____

Address: _____

_____

Budget: _____ Deposit: _____

Preferred Location		Property Needs	

Viewed	Suitable Properties

Notes: _____

_____

_____

_____

_____

_____

Property Sold		Costs
	VALUE	
	SOLD FOR	
	COMMISSION	

Individual Real Estate Log

Name: _____ Date: _____

Phone Number: _____ Email: _____

Address: _____

_____

Budget: _____ Deposit: _____

Preferred Location		Property Needs	

Viewed	Suitable Properties

Notes: _____

_____

_____

_____

_____

_____

Property Sold	Costs	
	VALUE	
	SOLD FOR	
	COMMISSION	

Individual Real Estate Log

Name: _____ Date: _____

Phone Number: _____ Email: _____

Address: _____

_____

Budget: _____ Deposit: _____

Preferred Location		Property Needs	

Viewed	Suitable Properties

Notes: _____

_____

_____

_____

_____

Property Sold	Costs	
	VALUE	
	SOLD FOR	
	COMMISSION	

Individual Real Estate Log

Name: _____ **Date:** _____

Phone Number: _____ **Email:** _____

Address: _____

_____

Budget: _____ **Deposit:** _____

Preferred Location		Property Needs	

Viewed	Suitable Properties

Notes: _____

_____

_____

_____

_____

_____

Property Sold		Costs
	VALUE	
	SOLD FOR	
	COMMISSION	

Individual Real Estate Log

Name: _____ Date: _____

Phone Number: _____ Email: _____

Address: _____

_____

Budget: _____ Deposit: _____

Preferred Location		Property Needs	

Viewed	Suitable Properties

Notes: _____

_____

_____

_____

_____

_____

_____

Property Sold	Costs	
	VALUE	
	SOLD FOR	
	COMMISSION	

Individual Real Estate Log

Name: _____ Date: _____

Phone Number: _____ Email: _____

Address: _____

_____

Budget: _____ Deposit: _____

Preferred Location		Property Needs	

Viewed	Suitable Properties

Notes: _____

_____

_____

_____

_____

_____

Property Sold	Costs	
	VALUE	
	SOLD FOR	
	COMMISSION	

Individual Real Estate Log

Name: _____ Date: _____

Phone Number: _____ Email: _____

Address: _____

Budget: _____ Deposit: _____

Preferred Location		Property Needs	

Viewed	Suitable Properties

Notes: _____

_____

_____

_____

_____

_____

_____

Property Sold	Costs	
	VALUE	
	SOLD FOR	
	COMMISSION	

Individual Real Estate Log

Name: _____ Date: _____

Phone Number: _____ Email: _____

Address: _____

_____

Budget: _____ Deposit: _____

Preferred Location		Property Needs	

Viewed	Suitable Properties

Notes: _____

_____

_____

_____

_____

_____

Property Sold	Costs	
	VALUE	
	SOLD FOR	
	COMMISSION	

Individual Real Estate Log

Name: _____ Date: _____

Phone Number: _____ Email: _____

Address: _____

_____

Budget: _____ Deposit: _____

Preferred Location		Property Needs	

Viewed	Suitable Properties

Notes: _____

_____

_____

_____

_____

Property Sold	Costs	
	VALUE	
	SOLD FOR	
	COMMISSION	

Individual Real Estate Log

Name: _____ Date: _____

Phone Number: _____ Email: _____

Address: _____

_____

Budget: _____ Deposit: _____

Preferred Location		Property Needs	

Viewed	Suitable Properties

Notes: _____

_____

_____

_____

_____

_____

Property Sold	Costs	
	VALUE	
	SOLD FOR	
	COMMISSION	

Individual Real Estate Log

Name: _____ Date: _____

Phone Number: _____ Email: _____

Address: _____
_____

Budget: _____ Deposit: _____

Preferred Location		Property Needs	

Viewed	Suitable Properties

Notes: _____
_____
_____
_____
_____
_____

Property Sold	Costs	
	VALUE	
	SOLD FOR	
	COMMISSION	

Individual Real Estate Log

Name: _____ Date: _____

Phone Number: _____ Email: _____

Address: _____

_____

Budget: _____ Deposit: _____

Preferred Location		Property Needs	

Viewed	Suitable Properties

Notes: _____

_____

_____

_____

_____

_____

Property Sold	Costs	
	VALUE	
	SOLD FOR	
	COMMISSION	

Individual Real Estate Log

Name: _____ Date: _____

Phone Number: _____ Email: _____

Address: _____

_____

Budget: _____ Deposit: _____

Preferred Location		Property Needs	

Viewed	Suitable Properties

Notes: _____

_____

_____

_____

_____

Property Sold	Costs	
	VALUE	
	SOLD FOR	
	COMMISSION	

Individual Real Estate Log

Name: _____ Date: _____

Phone Number: _____ Email: _____

Address: _____
_____

Budget: _____ Deposit: _____

Preferred Location		Property Needs	

Viewed	Suitable Properties

Notes: _____
_____
_____
_____
_____
_____

Property Sold	Costs	
	VALUE	
	SOLD FOR	
	COMMISSION	

Individual Real Estate Log

Name: _____ Date: _____

Phone Number: _____ Email: _____

Address: _____

_____

Budget: _____ Deposit: _____

Preferred Location		Property Needs	

Viewed	Suitable Properties

Notes: _____

_____

_____

_____

_____

_____

_____

Property Sold	Costs	
	VALUE	
	SOLD FOR	
	COMMISSION	

Individual Real Estate Log

Name: _____ Date: _____

Phone Number: _____ Email: _____

Address: _____

_____

Budget: _____ Deposit: _____

Preferred Location		Property Needs	

Viewed	Suitable Properties

Notes: _____

_____

_____

_____

_____

Property Sold	Costs	
	VALUE	
	SOLD FOR	
	COMMISSION	

Individual Real Estate Log

Name: _____ Date: _____

Phone Number: _____ Email: _____

Address: _____
_____

Budget: _____ Deposit: _____

Preferred Location		Property Needs	

Viewed	Suitable Properties

Notes: _____
_____
_____
_____
_____
_____
_____

Property Sold	Costs	
	VALUE	
	SOLD FOR	
	COMMISSION	

Individual Real Estate Log

Name: _____ Date: _____
Phone Number: _____ Email: _____
Address: _____
_____

Budget: _____ Deposit: _____

Preferred Location		Property Needs	

Viewed	Suitable Properties

Notes: _____
_____
_____
_____
_____
_____

Property Sold	Costs	
	VALUE	
	SOLD FOR	
	COMMISSION	

Individual Real Estate Log

Name: _____ Date: _____

Phone Number: _____ Email: _____

Address: _____

Budget: _____ Deposit: _____

Preferred Location		Property Needs	

Viewed	Suitable Properties

Notes: _____

_____

_____

_____

_____

_____

Property Sold	Costs	
	VALUE	
	SOLD FOR	
	COMMISSION	

Individual Real Estate Log

Name: _____ Date: _____

Phone Number: _____ Email: _____

Address: _____

_____

Budget: _____ Deposit: _____

Preferred Location		Property Needs	

Viewed	Suitable Properties

Notes: _____

_____

_____

_____

_____

_____

Property Sold	Costs	
	VALUE	
	SOLD FOR	
	COMMISSION	

Individual Real Estate Log

Name: _____ Date: _____

Phone Number: _____ Email: _____

Address: _____

Budget: _____ Deposit: _____

Preferred Location		Property Needs	

Viewed	Suitable Properties

Notes: _____

_____

_____

_____

_____

Property Sold	Costs	
	VALUE	
	SOLD FOR	
	COMMISSION	

Individual Real Estate Log

Name: _____ Date: _____

Phone Number: _____ Email: _____

Address: _____
_____

Budget: _____ Deposit: _____

Preferred Location		Property Needs	

Viewed	Suitable Properties

Notes: _____
_____
_____
_____
_____
_____

Property Sold	Costs	
	VALUE	
	SOLD FOR	
	COMMISSION	

Individual Real Estate Log

Name: _____ Date: _____

Phone Number: _____ Email: _____

Address: _____

_____

Budget: _____ Deposit: _____

Preferred Location		Property Needs	

Viewed	Suitable Properties

Notes: _____

_____

_____

_____

_____

Property Sold	Costs	
	VALUE	
	SOLD FOR	
	COMMISSION	

Individual Real Estate Log

Name: _____ Date: _____

Phone Number: _____ Email: _____

Address: _____
_____

Budget: _____ Deposit: _____

Preferred Location		Property Needs	

Viewed	Suitable Properties

Notes: _____
_____
_____
_____
_____
_____

Property Sold	Costs	
	VALUE	
	SOLD FOR	
	COMMISSION	

Individual Real Estate Log

Name: _____ Date: _____

Phone Number: _____ Email: _____

Address: _____

_____

Budget: _____ Deposit: _____

Preferred Location		Property Needs	

Viewed	Suitable Properties

Notes: _____

_____

_____

_____

_____

_____

Property Sold	Costs	
	VALUE	
	SOLD FOR	
	COMMISSION	

Individual Real Estate Log

Name: _____ Date: _____

Phone Number: _____ Email: _____

Address: _____

_____

Budget: _____ Deposit: _____

Preferred Location		Property Needs	

Viewed	Suitable Properties

Notes: _____

_____

_____

_____

_____

_____

Property Sold		Costs
	VALUE	
	SOLD FOR	
	COMMISSION	

Individual Real Estate Log

Name: _____ Date: _____

Phone Number: _____ Email: _____

Address: _____

Budget: _____ Deposit: _____

Preferred Location		Property Needs	

Viewed	Suitable Properties

Notes: _____

_____

_____

_____

_____

_____

Property Sold	Costs	
	VALUE	
	SOLD FOR	
	COMMISSION	

Individual Real Estate Log

Name: _____ Date: _____

Phone Number: _____ Email: _____

Address: _____

_____

Budget: _____ Deposit: _____

Preferred Location		Property Needs	

Viewed	Suitable Properties

Notes: _____

_____

_____

_____

_____

Property Sold	Costs	
	VALUE	
	SOLD FOR	
	COMMISSION	

Individual Real Estate Log

Name: _____ Date: _____

Phone Number: _____ Email: _____

Address: _____

_____

Budget: _____ Deposit: _____

Preferred Location		Property Needs	

Viewed	Suitable Properties

Notes: _____

_____

_____

_____

_____

Property Sold	Costs	
	VALUE	
	SOLD FOR	
	COMMISSION	

Individual Real Estate Log

Name: _____ Date: _____

Phone Number: _____ Email: _____

Address: _____

_____

Budget: _____ Deposit: _____

Preferred Location		Property Needs	

Viewed	Suitable Properties

Notes: _____

_____

_____

_____

_____

_____

Property Sold	Costs	
	VALUE	
	SOLD FOR	
	COMMISSION	

Individual Real Estate Log

Name: _____ Date: _____

Phone Number: _____ Email: _____

Address: _____

Budget: _____ Deposit: _____

Preferred Location		Property Needs	

Viewed	Suitable Properties

Notes: _____

_____

_____

_____

_____

_____

Property Sold	Costs	
	VALUE	
	SOLD FOR	
	COMMISSION	

Individual Real Estate Log

Name: _____ Date: _____

Phone Number: _____ Email: _____

Address: _____

_____

Budget: _____ Deposit: _____

Preferred Location		Property Needs	

Viewed	Suitable Properties

Notes: _____

_____

_____

_____

_____

_____

Property Sold	Costs	
	VALUE	
	SOLD FOR	
	COMMISSION	

Individual Real Estate Log

Name: _____ Date: _____

Phone Number: _____ Email: _____

Address: _____
_____

Budget: _____ Deposit: _____

Preferred Location		Property Needs	

Viewed	Suitable Properties

Notes: _____
_____
_____
_____
_____
_____

Property Sold	Costs	
	VALUE	
	SOLD FOR	
	COMMISSION	

Individual Real Estate Log

Name: _____ Date: _____

Phone Number: _____ Email: _____

Address: _____

_____

Budget: _____ Deposit: _____

Preferred Location		Property Needs	

Viewed	Suitable Properties

Notes: _____

_____

_____

_____

_____

_____

Property Sold	Costs	
	VALUE	
	SOLD FOR	
	COMMISSION	

Individual Real Estate Log

Name: _____ Date: _____

Phone Number: _____ Email: _____

Address: _____

Budget: _____ Deposit: _____

Preferred Location		Property Needs	

Viewed	Suitable Properties

Notes: _____
_____
_____
_____
_____
_____

Property Sold	Costs	
	VALUE	
	SOLD FOR	
	COMMISSION	

Individual Real Estate Log

Name: _____ Date: _____

Phone Number: _____ Email: _____

Address: _____

_____

Budget: _____ Deposit: _____

Preferred Location		Property Needs	

Viewed	Suitable Properties

Notes: _____

_____

_____

_____

_____

_____

Property Sold	Costs	
	VALUE	
	SOLD FOR	
	COMMISSION	

Individual Real Estate Log

Name: _____ Date: _____

Phone Number: _____ Email: _____

Address: _____

Budget: _____ Deposit: _____

Preferred Location		Property Needs	

Viewed	Suitable Properties

Notes: _____

_____

_____

_____

_____

_____

Property Sold	Costs	
	VALUE	
	SOLD FOR	
	COMMISSION	

Individual Real Estate Log

Name: _____ Date: _____

Phone Number: _____ Email: _____

Address: _____

_____

Budget: _____ Deposit: _____

Preferred Location		Property Needs	

Viewed	Suitable Properties

Notes: _____

_____

_____

_____

_____

_____

Property Sold	Costs	
	VALUE	
	SOLD FOR	
	COMMISSION	

Individual Real Estate Log

Name: _____ **Date:** _____

Phone Number: _____ **Email:** _____

Address: _____

Budget: _____ **Deposit:** _____

Preferred Location		Property Needs	

Viewed	Suitable Properties

Notes: _____

_____

_____

_____

_____

_____

Property Sold	Costs	
	VALUE	
	SOLD FOR	
	COMMISSION	

Individual Real Estate Log

Name: _____ Date: _____
Phone Number: _____ Email: _____
Address: _____
_____

Budget: _____ Deposit: _____

Preferred Location		Property Needs	

Viewed	Suitable Properties

Notes: _____
_____
_____
_____
_____

Property Sold	Costs	
	VALUE	
	SOLD FOR	
	COMMISSION	

Individual Real Estate Log

Name: _____ Date: _____

Phone Number: _____ Email: _____

Address: _____
_____

Budget: _____ Deposit: _____

Preferred Location		Property Needs	

Viewed	Suitable Properties

Notes: _____
_____
_____
_____
_____
_____

Property Sold	Costs	
	VALUE	
	SOLD FOR	
	COMMISSION	

Individual Real Estate Log

Name: _____ **Date:** _____

Phone Number: _____ **Email:** _____

Address: _____

Budget: _____ **Deposit:** _____

Preferred Location		Property Needs	

Viewed	Suitable Properties

Notes: _____

_____

_____

_____

_____

_____

Property Sold	Costs	
	VALUE	
	SOLD FOR	
	COMMISSION	

Individual Real Estate Log

Name: _____ Date: _____

Phone Number: _____ Email: _____

Address: _____
_____

Budget: _____ Deposit: _____

Preferred Location		Property Needs	

Viewed	Suitable Properties

Notes: _____
_____
_____
_____
_____
_____

Property Sold		Costs	
	VALUE		
	SOLD FOR		
	COMMISSION		

Individual Real Estate Log

Name: _____ Date: _____

Phone Number: _____ Email: _____

Address: _____

Budget: _____ Deposit: _____

Preferred Location		Property Needs	

Viewed	Suitable Properties

Notes: _____

_____

_____

_____

_____

Property Sold	Costs	
	VALUE	
	SOLD FOR	
	COMMISSION	

Individual Real Estate Log

Name: _____ Date: _____

Phone Number: _____ Email: _____

Address: _____

_____

Budget: _____ Deposit: _____

Preferred Location		Property Needs	

Viewed	Suitable Properties

Notes: _____

_____

_____

_____

_____

_____

Property Sold	Costs	
	VALUE	
	SOLD FOR	
	COMMISSION	

Individual Real Estate Log

Name: _____ Date: _____

Phone Number: _____ Email: _____

Address: _____

_____

Budget: _____ Deposit: _____

Preferred Location		Property Needs	

Viewed	Suitable Properties

Notes: _____

_____

_____

_____

_____

_____

Property Sold	Costs	
	VALUE	
	SOLD FOR	
	COMMISSION	

Individual Real Estate Log

Name: _____ Date: _____

Phone Number: _____ Email: _____

Address: _____
_____

Budget: _____ Deposit: _____

Preferred Location		Property Needs	

Viewed	Suitable Properties

Notes: _____
_____
_____
_____
_____
_____

Property Sold	Costs	
	VALUE	
	SOLD FOR	
	COMMISSION	

Individual Real Estate Log

Name: _____ Date: _____

Phone Number: _____ Email: _____

Address: _____

_____

Budget: _____ Deposit: _____

Preferred Location		Property Needs	

Viewed	Suitable Properties

Notes: _____

_____

_____

_____

_____

_____

Property Sold	Costs	
	VALUE	
	SOLD FOR	
	COMMISSION	

Individual Real Estate Log

Name: _____ Date: _____

Phone Number: _____ Email: _____

Address: _____

Budget: _____ Deposit: _____

Preferred Location		Property Needs	

Viewed	Suitable Properties

Notes: _____

_____

_____

_____

_____

Property Sold	Costs	
	VALUE	
	SOLD FOR	
	COMMISSION	

Individual Real Estate Log

Name: _____ Date: _____

Phone Number: _____ Email: _____

Address: _____

Budget: _____ Deposit: _____

Preferred Location		Property Needs	

Viewed	Suitable Properties

Notes: _____
_____
_____
_____
_____
_____

Property Sold	Costs	
	VALUE	
	SOLD FOR	
	COMMISSION	

Individual Real Estate Log

Name: _____ Date: _____

Phone Number: _____ Email: _____

Address: _____

_____

Budget: _____ Deposit: _____

Preferred Location		Property Needs	

Viewed	Suitable Properties

Notes: _____

_____

_____

_____

_____

_____

Property Sold	Costs	
	VALUE	
	SOLD FOR	
	COMMISSION	

Individual Real Estate Log

Name: _____ Date: _____

Phone Number: _____ Email: _____

Address: _____

_____

Budget: _____ Deposit: _____

Preferred Location		Property Needs	

Viewed	Suitable Properties

Notes: _____

_____

_____

_____

_____

_____

Property Sold	Costs	
	VALUE	
	SOLD FOR	
	COMMISSION	

Made in the USA
Las Vegas, NV
23 September 2021